JESUS,
the Bridge

by Melisa Calcote

Print information available on the last page

Rev. date: 07/22/2015

To order additional copies of this book, contact:
Xlibris
1-888-795-4274
www.Xlibris.com
Orders@Xlibris.com

This is dedicated to all my Family and
Christian Family who has always been
An encouragement and inspiration to me, and
Who have always been there for me.

Jesus is the Bridge

What is a bridge? It's a structure that allows people or vehicles to cross over a river, canal, or railway. We look at bridges as getting from one place to another, connecting us to the opposite side. In a way, Jesus is like a bridge that connects us to God. For it is through Jesus Christ that we are one with our God.

He is the Bridge in my life and yours that makes us whole and complete with our God. He is everything that we need. Through Jesus Christ, there is peace, love, joy, acceptance, understanding, loving kindness, perseverance, patience, and so much more. Through forgiveness of sins, He has given me this inner peace. It's a tranquil and quiet place where Love binds us together with our Lord God.

He gives me strength to face unavoidable obstacles in my daily walk. He has shed light in my life and in my heart to guide me through this earthly life. For I come into His presence with thanksgiving, and joy within my heart that He has restored unto me. He's my light and my salvation, the one who brought me peace. Jesus also helps to close the gap between God and us as He intercedes on our behalf when we come before God in prayer.

I know that God has a purpose for each and every one of us.
His purpose, the will of God, is that we love one another just as He loves us all.
John 3:16 "For God so loved the world, that He gave His one and only Son, that whoever believes in Him should not perish but have eternal life."

Psalms 138:8 – The Lord will fulfill His purpose for me;
your Love, O Lord, endures forever.

Let us build a bridge for others as we share the Love of God with all those around us.

Let's Build A Bridge

"Let's build a bridge, - you and me.
We'll take it one step at a time, one day at a time.

We'll build a friendship that is based on Jesus,
who is our foundation and start from the bottom up.
We'll began with getting to know each other, and
learn to include God in our conversation, as
He always wants to be a part of our lives,
and in our relationships.

We'll cross and conquer many obstacles that may get
in our way. We'll study the Word of God together
And He'll show us His purpose for our lives.
We'll grow in the Love for others as He helps us
break down walls of all kinds.

Let us build many bridges that will
connect to others All over the world.
Let us chip away the walls that separate us,
and let us become One in the Lord
as we share peace, joy, compassion,
and loving kindness to all.
Let's build a bridge today."

For God will never leave us nor forsake us,
And will never leave us stranded.
He will always be with us and help
Us to persevere through everything in life.

Isaiah 40:31 "but they who wait for the Lord
shall renew their strength, they shall mount
up with wings as eagles, they shall run and
not be weary, they shall walk and not faint."

Abounding Love

I sing to the Nations a new song
of forgiveness and Love, -an eternal love.
His Love is abounding, honest and true.
a Love of the Father who will
always be there to Love and nurture you.
To help you grow in so many ways
in an abounding love, and you will be amazed
of all the treasures He has in store for you.

Yes, sing to the Nations, All ye Earth,
rejoice in praise of a new birth.
The rebirth of your Faith
as you accept Him into your life.
For God Loves you, forgives you
and wants to be a part of your life
Today.

Sing to the Nations a new song.
A song of Joy and Thanksgiving
of the Love that He's given
to you.

Angels Unaware

He sits high above the rocks and trees up on a cliff looking down,
As he scans across the land and seas,
looking for anything out of the ordinary
That may bring trouble unaware.

And there, out on the ocean, He sees a ship in trouble.
Fighting against the mighty wind and rain, struggling with all his strain,
The captain takes hold of the wheel as he attempts to keep from flipping over.
Then all of a sudden, one of his shipmates fell overboard,
While trying to tie things down, yet the Captain was unaware.

He came swooping down from the heavens, for He knew it was not his time to go.
And without hesitation, goes diving into the water as Mother Nature gave it her all.
The shipmate was struggling to keep from being sucked down into the deep blue;
Then someone grabbed his hand and started guiding him back up to the surface.
Although he didn't know who or what was going on, he could not see his rescuer,
For the angel was invisible to him. But just as he caught his breath, and saw the ship
Not far away, started yelling to get the Captains attention; yet, when he called,
The captains Fog light suddenly got brighter and seemed to point into his direction.
Yes! He was spotted by the Captain, and he called the others to throw him the life raft.
They pulled him into safety, as finally the storm was subsiding and the howling winds
Winded down to a breeze.

The sailors were huddling together to take care of their mate;
Gave him a blanket and they all sat down on the deck.
Then the Captain gave a whistle that welcomed him back home,
To a crew who's like a family who looks after their own.
And the Captain was grateful that God had spared the life of his mate,
As he gives a big sigh of relief, and says to himself,
"Thank you Lord, for what you've done today."

The Angel, now standing above them at the top of the mainmast,
looks down to examine the view below. Reassured that all was right
He spreads his wings that were halfway dry, and mounted off in the
Heavens above.

Just one of many, that answers the call of saving the souls of God's children,
The Angels are there, and sometimes least of all we're unaware that they are in our presence.
Looking out over us, protecting us, and guiding us to safety.
And more importantly, noticing and recognizing when those who are saved,
Fall on bended knee, praying and praising God for whoever was looking over thee.

April Showers

Its morning, the trees are heavy with dew
Dripping from the leaves, as the fog rolls in.
The squirrels are no-where to be seen,
Waiting for it to pass.
The birds are taking cover
For they know what's coming.
And no sooner that the last one to perch on a limb,
The rain begins to come.
The clouds have opened the flood gates
As big drops of rain begin to fall,
Watering the earth, that is well needed;
To bring forth a new freshness in the air.
The rain stays for a while as it cleanses the ground
To bring new growth of all kinds of flowers,
Bushes and trees.
And as a glimmer of sunlight peeks through the clouds,
The flow of droplets ceases to be;
Only to bring forth the form of a rainbow
Reaching across the sky,
To share the sign of God's covenant that
He gave to you and me.

April showers, yes I see your
Sign of freshness and
A new beginning for me.

Beyond The Horizon

All your hopes and dreams
Can be found far beyond the sunset,
Far beyond the stars.
Over there, beyond the horizon,
Are the many answers to our prayers,
and answers to our questions.

For beyond the Horizon
And further than the eye can see,
Is the vast creation of our Lord and King.
All you have to do is say "Yes" to Him,
        "Yes, I Believe!"
Welcome Him into your heart today.
Welcome Him into your heart to stay.
For it is our fellowship with him
That makes it all worthwhile.

He the great Physician, the great I Am.
He is the Alpha and the Omega,
The Beginning and the End.
Far beyond the sunset, and far beyond the horizon
Into the vast beyond is where I long to be.
Closer to my Savior,
Wrapped in the arms of my Lord.

For all the treasures He has in store for me,
-        That I could not afford.
For His Love endures forever,
And He waits for us all to gather
There at the River of Life,
Where He brings New Hope and New Horizons.
Further than the eye can see
Deeper than the deepest ocean
And wider than the sea.

He is the New Horizon
The Light that shines for me.

Come To The Kingdom

Do you remember when you sensed that
you needed a change in life?
You felt a nudge coming from deep inside.
Do you remember what was going on in your life?
When you wanted something different, something new?

You wanted to make things better, make it right.
You realized that the life you were living just
seemed empty, like there was a void in your life.
Asking God for help, you had to step over your pride,
and humbly come before him in prayer,
to ask Him to come inside and be a part of your life.

"Lord, I want to be born again in you.
Let me repent of my sins too, for I need your forgiveness.
 and I need your Love and compassion to help me through.
Lord, please forgive me, and make me new, that I may serve you."

For it is through Him that we receive living water to all
who thirst for righteousness sake. It is through baptism
where our sins are washed away, and He fills us with His Spirit,
and "Yes" He's here to stay.

All you have to do is: "Ask, and you will receive,
Seek and you shall find. Knock and the door shall be opened
to eternal life through Jesus Christ our Lord."

Come With Me

Through His grace, and through His Love,
Our Father from above is calling to you and to me.
Come with me, come and see
what I have to set you free.
Free from all your sins from the past.

Walk with me, talk with me.
Come and share your life with me;
For with you I long to be.
Come with me.
Take my hand, Take a stand,
Take a start, and be a part
of my Almighty Plan.

Come with me, come and be
All you can be, for through my Love
you are free to be who you really are.

For through my grace, and through my Love,
you can embrace from above,
all power to overcome obstacles of this race.

Walk with me, talk with me.
Come and share your life with me;
For with you I long to be.
Come with me.

Come with me, come and see
What I have to set you free.
Come receive all the Love
I have for thee.

Delivered

As He delivered the Israelites out from Egypt,
He will also deliver you from any unforeseen situations.
For all through creation as you have seen,
Jesus Christ is the foundation of our Faith,
-            Who is on the scene
to help us fight against all temptation.
For he will bring us to pastures green
Where He leads us with expectation.
Where He will bring us with anticipation
into the Glory of his Love.
Where, thru His Grace and compassion,
He brings us peace and inspiration
Through salvation of our soul.

Through His mercy in those we meet,
He brings compassion through times of defeat.
With loving arms reaching out to thee
And caring hearts to show us the way,
Let us all be disciples to help deliver those
in times of need.

Down The Road

In life, we never know whether
We're coming or going,
For life always throws different
Obstacles in our path.
But then, that's when we have to decide
The correct way to go,
To the left or to the right
And sometimes further into the night.
Not knowing what's ahead we trudge on.
Sometimes we end up praying for guidance
To help us do the right thing,
For further down the road
We might be able to help
Someone with a heavy load.
Further down the road
God guides us thru the different highways
That sometimes we wonder
How do we get through it all?
But through it all, as we go further down the road
We know He will always be with us
Through life's Highway.

Fishers Of Men

The day was perfect, especially for fishing.
We were out on the water in the early morning,
 in anticipation for the catch of the day.
Willing to wait patiently for the fish to come our way,
going from spot to spot at just the right time
to come upon a school of Reds or Trout.
It was just cool enough to bring the fish out.

As we chat about everything that's going on in our lives,
 we watch the current and to see where the wind is blowing.
You could see the way the water ripples, to where the fish are going.
And looking up above, the birds fly overhead,
in a certain direction where others are diving into the deep.
Following the birds is the best sign to know where to go for the best catch to keep.

I'm reminded of the disciples, how Jesus came to them.
When he said "I will make you fishers of men."
How Jesus patiently taught them the word of God,
How he taught them through the parables
and blessed them through the spiritual realm.
We serve a mighty God, - for He is at the helm
of the ship that we're traveling on.
And He encourages us all to be fishers of men.

Forever

Butterflies and bumblebees,
How they make such harmony
Through creation of this world
in transformation to new life
in shedding of the old ways
to be suddenly changed
from cocoon into a beautiful butterfly
that's been set free.

Bumblebees come to flowers you see
as they receive a part to feed.
Flowers resound with sweetness in the air
as they long to share
their sweet fragrance everywhere.

Like the butterflies and bumblebees,
How they make such harmony.
Though, to me it seems to be
showing God's great love for me.
How He's changed my life, you see,
For I'm now forever free.

He's forever my Savior,
forever my Lord.
He's forever with me,
to uphold and strengthen me.
Butterflies and bumblebees remind me
of His gracious Love for me.

Glory

I hear Him calling in the night as
I awake to the sound of my name.
I suddenly stop and listen to what
seems to explain the urging of the spirit.

His voice is loud like lightning,
streaking across the night sky, as
I feel the rumble of the earth beneath me,
and began to wonder why.
But it's the voice I hear falling on my ear
that seems so powerful and mighty.
His voice can shake the desert, and
at the same time, through a whisper, make
you shiver with goose bumps that seem to appear.
And I know that I hear His voice,
Proclaiming to sing and rejoice,
for the heavens shake with glory
and majestically in one voice cries,
"Glory".

Psalm 29

He Is Coming

Hosanna, Hosanna to Jesus Christ our Lord.
Hosanna to the King.
For He came to bring salvation to all.
Let us come to Him rejoicing.
Let us come to Him in song.
Lay down the palm branches before Him.
Let us come and adore Him.

God loved us so much that He gave
His only Son as a sacrifice for our sins,
that through our redemption,
we can have new life in Him.

Hosanna to Jesus Christ our Lord.
Let us give thanks and praise to our Father
for His son Jesus Christ,
who was willing to pay the price for our souls.

Make way for the coming of the Lord.
Make way for the King of kings
for He is Jesus Christ our King.

Through his death, He took our burdens.
In his rising, he set us free.
Through God's grace, we have salvation
through all eternity.

Make way for the coming of the Lord
into your life today.
Open the door of your heart and
welcome him in to stay.

He's Lord Of Us All

Dark clouds come rolling in
As they began to cover the sun.
Birds in the air,
Flying to and fro to their nest.
Squirrels scattering here and there
Gathering nuts to bring to their lair.
And I hear the thunder
Bellowing in the clouds
As it begins to sprinkle
All around.
And as if someone pulled a shade,
The sun disappears behind
The darkness of the clouds
As the rains start coming down,
Watering the bushes, trees and flowers
Filtering into the ground.

As the tears of heaven fall
For the unsaved of this world
And prayers are lifted up
For protection of unseen things unfurled.
Little do we know
Of the things that lie ahead,
Like the storms that come and go,
Or will there be sunshine instead?

Now I see the rain falling down
Hard and fast as the
Lightning streaks across the sky.
My thoughts and my prayers
I often share
"God, will you be there?"
Then as the hard rain
Slows down to a crawl,
The clouds begin to move away,
A beam of sunlight shines through
That seems to say,
"He's Lord of us ALL.
And He'll always be there."

Hold Me Close, Lord

Hold me close, Lord,
Never let me go, Lord.
You are my strength and my shield,
Unto you I will yield.
You lift me up in your glory,
And your loving eyes I see.

Hold me close, Lord,
Never let me go, Lord.
Knowing you will never leave me
Nor never forsake me,
Even through trials and tribulations.
Through your Love and compassion
You bring me peace and understanding
and set me upon this Rock, where I'm standing.
Yes, I'm standing closer to thee.

Hold me close, Lord,
Never let me go, Lord.
Through you there is peace and contentment
For in you, there is satisfaction of my soul.
You, Lord, have made me whole.

Hold me close, Lord.
Never let me go, Lord.
For you hold me in your arms in my dreams
And rock me to sleep, though it seems.
Hearing the tune of 'Rock of Ages'
As I'm flying through the pages of time….
You wake me with a joy and celebration
And give me constant inspiration
That leads me through this life I go
although I'm never alone.

Hold me close, Lord,
Never let me go, Lord.
For I never want to be without you.

Holy Ground

Holy Ground, I'm standing on Holy Ground,
Where the Spirit of my Lord Bids me come.
I will follow where He leads,
I bow down before the throne of my Lord.

Holy Ground, -where He stands in the midst,
The clouds are all around,
Where I'm standing on Holy Ground.

In the silence, I hear His voice.
In my heart, the tender touch of His hand.
In my soul, I hear Him calling.
In my life, I know He's there
     All the way.

In His presence I long to stay.
His Spirit sustains me
Through this journey,
Where He leads me
Through all eternity.

I Am

I am many things, many places,
many faces, creatures and creation.
I am the colors of the rainbow that
brings hope for the morrow.
I am the tear of someone's eye
that finds joy after sorrow.

I am the lioness with her young.
I am each and every creature and beyond.
I am in the streams that flow down the mountain.
I am in the dawn and dusk of your days.
I bring you the hope of a new tomorrow.
of the stars on which you gaze.

I am in the rain that falls on your face.
I am everything you wish to embrace.

I am Faith, Hope and Love.
Everything above and beyond.
Come let me share with you who I AM.

I Knew You When....

I knew you when you were little,
I knew you when you weren't even born,
and even before the earth was formed.
I knew you when you were just an idea
forming within me, as a child of mine.

Oh how I want to show you so much,
I will show you how the world came to be
I will show you my love for thee.

I knew you when I came into existence,
for I was the first, and will be the last.
I will show you how to love your brother.
I will care for you, nurture you,
encourage you, and help you to grow.
As I am one with the father,
so will I be one with you.

I Send You Forth

They were all together in this room
In worship and prayer as one.
Everything was about to change
As Jesus Christ, His Son
Had interceded for them.
Then a mighty wind came from nowhere
And filled each one with His Spirit.
And all of them could swear
They weren't sure what just happened.

Then their feelings, they wanted to share
Were lost in words nobody could compare.
They were all speaking in different tongues.
They looked at each other wondering what's next,
Then they realized it was real easy
And not even complex.
For as one, they had prayed for guidance,
And the Lord answered their prayers.
For they knew what needed to be done,
And they would have to work together as one,
To complete the mission God had given them.
To them, it was like a rare gem
That you just wanted to share with the world.
So they nodded their good-byes
To depart to their own country,
And everything began to unfurl
As they began to spread the Good News
Of Jesus Christ our Lord.

I Will Wait On The Lord

Where he leads me, I will follow.
When he says, I will stay.
When he tells me, I will wait
patiently for Him.

Yes, I will wait upon the Lord earnest, patiently.
I will wait upon the Lord, anticipating in Him.

Though my yearning grows to be with my Lord eternally.
Through the wisdom of His words, I wait to receive.
When my way groweth near to the heart of my Lord,
though the trials I've endured, in Him, I am secure.
And I shall wait upon the Lord.

Through all trials and tribulations
He leads me through the storm.
And there is celebration through
salvation of my Lord.
I will wait on the Lord.

Through His inspiration, He leads me through this life,
and there is consolation in my Lord Jesus Christ.
When my life groweth near, my Lord lingers here.
For He brings me to salvation into the presence of his Love.
I'm waiting on my Lord.

Imitation

He went about doing good – for God was with him
    And he'll be with you too.

Through God's mercy, he saved us.
He cleansed us through the blood of the lamb and
He renews us with the Holy Spirit.

Through his death, he took our burdens,
    In his rising, he set us free.
In his Faithfulness, he gave new Life,
A commitment he made to you and me.

In his Gentleness, he gives us Peace
Through his Peace, he gave us Understanding.
Through his Understanding, he gave us Wisdom.
In his Wisdom, he gave us Patience
    and Endurance
Through his Endurance, he gave us a Faith -
    A Faith so strong ….

In Gods' Spirit, he heals and makes us whole-
    spituually and physically.
Yet, through his love, he is Our Comforter,
    Our Provider,
        Our Strength in need.
He Encourages and Teaches us
And shows us how to be more like Him.

He's the Son of the Living God,
He's Jesus Christ our King.

He claims us as his own, for our Father waits
for us to come home to be in his loving care;
to share our lives with him,
to communicate with him through
His word and in prayer.

In An Instant

Through the raging storms of life,
when things seem to go awry.
When you think there's no other way
to make it all go away.
There is Hope deep inside
that not even we can hide,
that makes us realize
And notice the tears in His eyes.

But if we stop for a moment
and bow down at his feet.
Bring everything to Him.
Satan has already been defeated.
The fleeting pain will depart
when you welcome him into your heart.

And in an instant of time,
You will realize......
how precious life is,
when you come to conclusion
how much "He" Loves you so.

In an instant, when all stands still,
through the power of the Holy Spirit,
He does restore new life
at the command of my Fathers' will.

In Passing....

Walking in His Word
Living day by day,
He fills me with His love
As I grow in His way.

Every blessing He gives I cherish
Every day He gives I Live
that I may give each day to Him.
Everyone I meet in passing,
Everyone I tell of Him
Of all His many blessings
That He's bestowed on me.

And in passing, as I see Him
In many faces, lives, and lifestyles,
In the past thru many situations
Through the many miles.

In passing, I see how He touches
Through healing, love and compassion,
Those who reach out to Him.
In passing, I feel His presence
from those who have touched my life,
in so many ways, through so many friends
who has been there – transcends.

In passing, I see the horizon.
How He touches the earth to
bring new life.

And in passing, He flows into my heart
To bring new life within.
In passing…..

Life Is Worth Living

It was a place in time
Where He bids me come
When He calls my name.
There's no reason or rhyme
Nor where I come from,
For He's always the same.
The clock no longer chimes,
As time stands still
For when I am there within His presence
At my Fathers' will.

When He bids me come
At the sound of His voice,
My heart reaches out,
My soul rejoices.
For through His compassion
He holds my hand,
Through the love of a caring friend.

Within His presence, He fills me anew,
Gives me strength and direction
As through His power
I will serve you.
I will be your shoulder to lean on.
I will do everything I can
To lend a helping hand.
I will be your friend indeed.
I will help you lead
A life worth living.
For through the renewing power of His Spirit,
We can live a joyful life of giving.
For through a loving God,
Life is worth Living.

Lord, Show Us the Way

As moments pass by in living our lives,
We wonder which way to go.
Which way to go we say.
Doing what we think is best
Or living how we think God would approve,
But sometimes we wander away.

But he is there, as we sometimes know unaware,
Nudging, and prodding, trying to pull
us completely out of God's reach.
Throwing obstacles in our way;
Liars, cheaters, killers and thieves.
Lurking in the shadows and ready to pounce
He's waiting in the valley of the shadow of doubt.
Tempting and teasing,

How could we ever be accepted again?
Because of the webs we weave?
The one thing Satan doesn't realize and
Seems to never will,
Is how much our God Loves us,
And will always forgive.
For He knows we've made wrong choices
Since the beginning of time.
For He'll never turn us away
When we're down on our knees to pray,
Repenting of our sins, and
Asking "Lord, show us the way."

Morning Flight

She sits there upon the mountaintop
snowcapped from the night before,
to see what there is in store
through all the beauty of all creation
that expands there before her.
As she glares into the endless scene
of mountains far beyond,
rolling towards the whitecaps of the sea,
listening to the morning song
as this was her daily routine.

All of a sudden, she stretches her wings
and looks up into heaven, it seems,
as she raises her head, and lets out a screech.
Turning around and looking in all directions
as if giving an inspection
of any predators that might come her way.
She pauses a moment, then takes position
as if she is on a mission.
And in an effortless lift, stretching her arms,
she rises towards the heavens to reach
towards the great beyond.

And as the sun begins to rise in the east,
slowly increasing in acceleration
heading towards her destination,
she begins her search for a feast.

As she glides along through the air,
with the wind beneath her wings,
she catches scenes from down below.
Blessed with the gift of newborn within the nest,
She gives nothing but the best
as she provides in nurturing her young.

So as she returns to her offspring with meal in tow,
the male eagle steps away for her to feed their young.
Not to be too far away, but to be the bold and strong.
Protector of the nest, and proud to be where he belongs.
　Nestled near the nest, the guardian of the sky,
　　- They're the bold, the beautiful,
　　　as created by our God on High.

Behold, look and see, what our Father has made for thee,
　All creation that's all around you,
　　the freedom HE gives to learn, to grow,
　　　and to be all that you can be.

Rainbows

The colors of the Rainbow
Are so beautiful to see.
It reminds me of the Hope for tomorrow
God has given to me.

A hope for new beginnings,
For new life of a baby
And new life for our souls.
Rainbows give us hope every day
That you will always be with us
In all our many ways.

Your love is all sufficient and all that I need
To love and serve you, Lord and
The grace and honor of thee.
The colors of the Rainbow,
Yes, they're so beautiful to see.
It reminds me of your covenant you made to us,
And gives me new hope, new joys,
New goals in life, that will
Give glory and honor to thee!

You are the hope of tomorrow
That I may always Love and serve thee!

Searching

There was a teenager who walked into a church
with questions, and answers worth searching.
As he walked down the aisle
and discovered to his surprise,
was a young man there, about his age and size.

He stood and greeted him with a handshake and smile,
"How are you doing today?" he replied,
realizing, in his heart, he had something on his mind.

"A little confused," the teenager said,
"I have many questions about something I've read.
Where I've been staying and people I've met,
Somehow, seems to me, of where I've been led."
Without hesitation and after a big breath,
the teenager went on to ask,
"Hey man, what's up with this
you all call this Master Plan?
There's something here I don't quite understand,"
he said as he began to pace back and forth,
wondering inside, if it was all worth his being there.
"I'm not quite sure what to make of this, you see.
I grew up around the roughest part of town.
So you see, I wanna know what's really going down."

The young man understood where he was coming from,
for he once knew what it was like
growing up on the other side of town.

Although, he had moved away not too long ago,
in search for whom he really was.
He came to this church where the teenager now stands,
also questioning about this master plan.
"Man, you're in the right place for what you seek.
For it is only through God where you will find
all the answers of the many questions in mind."

"So where is this book that I am told, that holds
all these mysteries? That, I want to know."
The young man picked up a bible there in the pew.
He turned to one of the gospels, that, for sure, he knew
would hold the key of the many mysteries.
And finally the teenager sat down beside him
hungry for the knowledge and
eager to fill the emptiness inside him.

Sonshine

Sunshine, light of the fire in the sky,
Shining down upon the earth
Which God had given new birth
Of the whole human race.
He treasures us of our worth,
-            And that we embrace.

Sunshine, that shines so brightly deep inside me,
The light that is embedded into my soul,
Brings forth all the gifts He has given to me,
And He reached down into my life and made me whole.

He's the Light that shines for me and
Brings all things into the Light.
And His rays are as far as I can see,
Even into the midst of the night.
As He brings me into sight,
It brings me down on bended knee,
That I shall worship and glorify thee.

Sunshine, light of my world,
Shine in my heart always,
Stay with me, and guard over me,
And protect me from the dangers of this world.
Son of God, my Lord Jesus Christ,
You are my life, and
I will serve and glorify thee.

He's the Sonshine of my life.

Spread Your Wings and Fly!

He was there on the table across from me
I watched him as he fluttered his wings and
He walked about on the table.
Then he looked straight at me
As if this bird actually knew me?
He started talking to me in his own language
although I did not understand a word.
I wondered what he was trying to say.
The more I watched this bird,
the more he started to stretch out his wings;
as if he was trying to tell me something.
Something of great importance.

The next day, he floated down to the table and
stood there watching me.
Then He started to sing such sweet music.
And he stretched out his wings and he walked
around on the table with such determination.
And the thought came across to me as if it came
directly from the tiny mind of this little bird,
"Spread Your Wings and Fly."

God seems to talk to us in several ways,
Through so many people, and through
the many situations we approach in our lifetime.
But this bird seemed to tell me,
"Spread Your Wings and Fly."
"Spread your Love to all those around you.
Spread the Love of our Lord into every situation
that life throws into your pathway. Be who you were
meant to be. Live life to the fullest, live it strong.

Live like today were to be your last day here on earth.
But also live it for God.
    Be spontaneous.   Be brave.
       Be courageous.   Be Loving.
Be at peace with yourself and with others around you.
Love others as you would want to be loved.
Be all that you can be. Life is too short.
You never know what tomorrow will bring.
Live life to the fullest, for in my heart this little bird sings
A tune of Love, Joy and Happiness.
And the Hope for tomorrow.

For Jesus is the Christ and
He lives Today for you and me.

"Spread Your Wings and Fly."

Stop To Smell The Roses

There may be times when everyday life gets so hectic,
you don't get to slow down a bit.
But we must remember to stop – and put everything on pause.
To notice the little things that God has done for us.

To watch the sun setting in the west as the colors
blend into the dusk of the night. To see the multitude
of stars in the sky reminds me of the days of creation
as I wonder in the awe of His touch.
To watch the squirrels playing in the trees or
To listen to the waves of the sea.
To watch the changing of the seasons
When the flowers began to bloom; when the trees
come awake after their winter sleep and when
you smell the aroma of the roses in their brilliant colors.

And I stop and think, "If God did all this for me,
He really does Loves us all. So I stop to enjoy
the beauty of thy creation!"

That's My Boy

As we prepare our hearts for the birth of our Savior,
Let us be mindful of how He must have felt.

"That's my boy," He said to the Angels,
Watch over him and keep him in your loving care.
I look forward to talking to him,
and watching him grow up into a loving son.
He'll grow up in a loving family, you know."

"He'll learn the trade of a carpenter and work with his hands.
He'll learn the tenderness of his mothers' heart,
and yes, he'll understand. That's my boy.
I see him in the temple talking to the elders.
I hear him through his prayers as he talks to me each day.
And I will put into his heart a loving and
gentle soul that people will get to know."

"That's my boy. He'll bring something new to the people.
Something they won't understand at first.
He'll show them how much I Love them,
and how much I care."

"That's my boy!"

The Chase

Ruffling through the leaves and running up the trees
we find him scouting for nuts for his dinner.
He runs down to the ground as he follows the acorns falling down,
Hopeful of gathering all them up to bring back to his burrow.

But, there, at the edge of the bushes,
lies waiting is Simon, the Siamese cat.
Waiting – patiently for his prey.

Rigby, the squirrel, does not see him at first,
for he's gathering as many as he can in his mouth and paws.
Then he stops, looks and listens, for he was sure
that he heard a crunching of leaves close by.
Just as he glances over to the bush, Simon leaps out at him.

Rigby drops everything and darts up the tree
with no hesitation of looking back to see
Simon on his bushy tail trying to snatch him
before he reached the tree.
But he failed to seize him at that moment.
Instead, Simon runs after the lean, wild squirrel
scurrying straight up the tree behind him.

Rigby stays as far ahead of Simon as he can
to give him a fighting chance of staying alive.
He jumps from limb to limb going higher and higher
with Simon almost right behind him trying his hardest to
stay up with the scrawny squirrel.

But Rigby seems to go even faster flinting about
        on the edge of limbs making his way
        all the way to the top of the tree.
As for Simon, he almost made it that far,
 just to jump to a somewhat sturdy limb only
to wobble in place, this forces Simon to retreat
back down the tree only to save one of his nine lives.

But he doesn't go far, only to rest for a while, and wait.
Yes, Wait – patiently again for the chance to catch that
scrawny 'Rigby' squirrel, who now sits quietly in his rest haven
at the top of the tree nibbling on another acorn,
and snickering at the cat below.

The Power Within

It is night and the full moon is out in the starry sky.
There's a cool breeze in the air as I sit here alone.
I hear the crickets in the grass and the traffic coming and going.
As I listen to the crickets, my mind starts to relax from a hard days' work.

There is calmness in my heart, -
No worries, no problems,
An assurance that everything is well.
There is an overcoming power deep
within me that absorbs all these things
and gives me this new, refreshed feeling.
It has a soothing affect on my spirit, and sets me free.

The power within guides me through
every hour of the day.
I have Faith that it will always be there for me,
for the Holy Spirit is my Friend,
my Healer, Comforter and Guide.
He is my light to eternal life.

Today

I wait patiently in my room in prayer to you.
listening for your voice to give me your instruction, Lord.
I pray reverently every day to you for guidance in my
daily life that I live for you Now – Today.

Today, I surrender everything to you, Lord.
You helped me make it through everything I've been through.
You accepted me back into your fold, and redeemed my soul.

Today, I will start believing in myself more because
He believes in me and has a purpose for my life.
Only He knows what the future holds, but
I know that He will guide me in all things that I do,
And steer me into the right direction of where He wants me to be.

Today, I will befriend someone and help them along the way,
for life is harsh enough to live in this world.
That doesn't mean we don't have to be in the world,
but of the world as children of God as we journey through this life together.

Let me be a light to others today, and share God's love with them.
Let my character show love, peace, joy and understanding
towards all who come my way.

Use me, dear Lord, where you want me to be,
Guide me in everything I do and say, and let my life
Be an instrument of your Love.

Today, I AM Yours, Lord God.
        But not just for Today, but FOREVER.

Tree Of Life

We are one, yet many
And yes there are plenty.
Each one of us is like a tree,
-a part of the Tree of Life.
He filled us with His Spirit
That we may work together as one,
Yet He made each one of us different
And many gifts He gave each one,
That we may use them to
Love and serve each other.
And we come together as one
To glorify and praise Jesus Christ, His son.
He gave each one a gift
That we may share in love
And compassion to others.
That in our giving and living together as one,
We may also Love our sisters and brothers
As we Love and serve our Lord Jesus Christ,
His Son.

Unconditional Love

It's a time of rejoicing, a time of preparation
and a time of expectation as we look forward
to the moment of his birth.

We come to the manger this season with expectation,
joy, hope, and love of our Lord who has come into our lives.
Let us come to the manger in humbleness and awe of the
wonder and greatness of the almighty God, who loves us so.

I look to the heavens, the work of thy hands,
the moon and the stars above;
that were established into place and
set into motion through his greatness thereof.
I look to the stars, far, far above;
from where He undoubtedly reaches
down to us with unconditional love.

Through his birth, our Father built this bridge
so that we may be connected with him as
we cross over into the presence of his glory
and come before him in the celebration
of his birth as we renew our faith in Him.

Walking With My Savior

Walking with my Savior day to day,
Sharing in the love he bestowed my way.

He showed me Love that I share with you.
He gave me Peace – a peace within my heart.
He gave me Joy, and a voice to sing of
His Glory, His honor, and life eternally.

Walking with my Savior day by day,
I see the touch of the Masters hand
In all who I see, and those who need his love.
Walking with my Savior day by day,
Reaching out as a helping hand on the road,
Helping those with a heavy load.
I see the love of God coming back to me
And in the ones I meet along the way.

"Continue your walk in my spirit, child,
Sow the seeds of your faith with those who pray,
And let them know that I will be with them always.
As you share my words of wisdom with them all,
Be strong for them as you pray."

Walking with my Savior day to day,
Sharing in the love he bestowed on me.

He showed me Love that I share with you.
He showed me grace, a grace so pure and
He gave me a place in the Glory of God.
He showed me a way to share with you,
All of my love and the Love of God.

Welcome To My World

Welcome to my World
Please come in and stay
Don't be afraid,
Please don't run away.
I welcome you indeed
And no, I will not mislead,
For this is your destiny
To be a part of Me,
That I shall be within you,
To guide and protect too,
In all the things you do.

Welcome to my World,
I made it just for you,
All the cosmos were hurled
Into place at just the right time
At just the right moment
So that you would know
That through the atonement
How much I Love you so.

When My Jesus Died

When my Jesus died,
He died for you and me,
He died to set us free.

When my Jesus died,
he went down to the grave
and took all our sins away.
Yet he rose again
so now He lives today.

When my Jesus died,
he gave his life for me
to give a gift of grace
for all life eternally.

So Jesus is my Lord, He's the Savior
He's my King.
For when my Lord Jesus died,
he made a way for us to come home
through repentance, forgiveness,
oh how the angels sing.

For each time one of His children
accepts Jesus into their hearts to stay,
all the hosts of the heavens and the
angels sing for Jesus Christ is King.